S0-BFB-799

Windows® XP

FOR

DUMMIES®

Pocket Edition

Based on Windows® XP For Dummies®

by Andy Rathbone

WILEY

Wiley Publishing, Inc.

Windows® XP For Dummies®, Pocket Edition

Published by
Wiley Publishing, Inc.
111 River Street
Hoboken, NJ 07030
www.wiley.com

About the Author

Andy Rathbone started geeking around with computers in 1985 when he bought a boxy CP/M Kaypro 2X with lime-green letters. Like other budding nerds, he soon began playing with null-modem adapters, dialing up computer bulletin boards, and working part-time at Radio Shack.

In between playing computer games, he served as editor of the *Daily Aztec* newspaper at San Diego State University. After graduating with a comparative literature degree, he went to work for a bizarre underground coffee-table magazine that sort of disappeared.

Andy began combining his two main interests, words and computers, by selling articles to a local computer magazine. During the next few years, he started ghostwriting computer books for more-famous computer authors, as well as writing several hundred articles about computers for technoid publications like *Supercomputing Review, CompuServe Magazine, ID Systems, DataPro,* and *Shareware*.

In 1992, Andy and *DOS For Dummies* author/legend Dan Gookin teamed up to write *PCs For Dummies*. Andy subsequently wrote the award-winning *Windows For Dummies* series, *Upgrading & Fixing PCs For Dummies, MP3 For Dummies,* and many other *For Dummies* books.

Today, he has more than 15 million copies of his books in print, which have been translated into more than 30 languages.

Andy lives with his most-excellent wife, Tina, and their cat in Southern California. He wants a new LCD panel monitor for his main computer, but then the cat wouldn't have anyplace to sleep. Feel free to drop by his Web site at www.andyrathbone.com.

Publisher's Acknowledgments

We're proud of this book; please send us your comments through our online registration form located at www.dummies.com/register/.

Some of the people who helped bring this book to market include the following:

Acquisitions, Editorial, and Media Development

Project Editors: Kim Darosett, Nicole Haims

Technical Editor: Lee Musick

Editorial Manager: Stephanie Corby

Cartoons: Rich Tennant, www.the5thwave.com

Production

Project Coordinator: Michael Sullivan

Layout and Graphics: Carrie Foster, Michael Sullivan

Proofreader: Laura Albert, Sossity Smith

Special Help: Jan Withers, Zoe Wykes

Publishing and Editorial for Technology Dummies

Richard Swadley, Vice President and Executive Group Publisher

Andy Cummings, Vice President and Publisher

Mary C. Corder, Editorial Director

Publishing for Consumer Dummies

Diane Graves Steele, Vice President and Publisher

Joyce Pepple, Acquisitions Director

Composition Services

Gerry Fahey, Vice President of Production Services

Debbie Stailey, Director of Composition Services

Contents at a Glance

Introduction

● ●

*W*elcome to *Windows XP For Dummies, Pocket Edition!* You've heard about the Windows XP operating system from Microsoft and possibly encountered it face-to-face on a computer. But have you really found your way around it yet? With the help of this book, you can change your entire computing XPerience. Get it? XP? XPerience?

If you're eager to hop into the new stuff Windows XP has in store for you (plus get some great hands-on computing know-how), simply thumb through this book to pick up a few chunks of useful information. You'll also get a quick tour of XP's new interface and features. In other words, you're in the right place to find out precisely what all the hullabaloo is about.

About This Book

You won't find any fancy computer jargon in this book. Instead, you find subjects like these, discussed in plain old English:

- ✔ Maneuvering through the new user interface and discovering new features
- ✔ Making Windows XP work again when it's misbehaving
- ✔ Getting high-tech with Windows XP's multimedia features
- ✔ Setting up user accounts for everyone in your household

There's nothing to memorize and nothing to learn. Just turn to the right page, read the brief explanation, and walk through the world knowing that you've seen the future of home computing. Okay, well, maybe this book doesn't do anything *quite* that dramatic. But the second you take Windows XP out of the box and install it, you can amaze your friends and family with the little nuggets of information you've already discovered in this book.

How to Use This Book

This book is as versatile as it is useful. Use the Contents at a Glance to quickly locate information by topic and then mix and match the following ways of reading the book to go along with your mood:

- ✔ **Read the book from cover-to-cover:** If you prefer to read straight through from front to back, sharpen your pencil so that you can take some notes in the margins.

- ✔ **Pick a part and run with it:** If you want to know about a specific feature, pick the part on that topic and start reading until you've satisfied your curiosity. Who am I to thwart your individuality?

- ✔ **Thumb through:** Scan the book until your eyes land on something that you find particularly scintillating.

- ✔ **Use the book as a mousepad:** Or a coaster. Or a Frisbee. Keep the book around just in case you need to find some information on the fly after you've installed Windows XP and gotten it running.

Keep in mind that this book is a short *reference* to
Windows XP's new features. It's not designed to teach
you how to use Windows XP like an expert, heaven
forbid. Instead, this book dishes out enough bite-sized
chunks of information so that you won't have to relearn
Windows basics just to use Windows XP.

And What about You?

Well, chances are that you have a computer that came
with Windows XP installed on it already. Or maybe
you're upgrading. Maybe you know Windows pretty
well already, and you also know what you want to do
with your computer. What you don't know is how
Windows XP's newest bells and whistles can help (or
hamper) your plans.

Note: Windows XP comes in two basic versions:
Windows XP Home and Windows XP Professional.
Chances are, you'll use Windows XP Home, the version
designed for homes and small businesses.

How This Book Is Organized

This book contains four parts. Here are the categories
(the envelope, please):

Part 1: Getting to Know Windows XP

This book starts with the basics and explains all the
Windows XP stuff that everybody thinks you already
know — like how the funky new Start button and
taskbar work and how to use My Computer. You also
find out about Windows XP's new activation process.

Maybe the most important thing this part does is show you where to turn to get help using Windows XP. Find out how to use Microsoft's resources in addition to the powerful help features already installed with Windows XP.

Part II: Discovering Windows XP and Multimedia

Windows XP leaps onto the screen with a snappy beat and overly excited videos. But how do you make the darn thing do something *useful?* Here, you find ways to overcome the frustratingly playful tendencies of Windows XP and force it to sweep leaves off the driveway or empty the dishwasher. Turn here for information on playing music CDs, MP3s and WMAs, and movies.

Part III: Setting Up a Windows XP Network at Home

Find out how to set up user accounts for every member of the family, even Fido if you're so inclined. And if you're interested in creating a home network that runs XP, you're in luck. Find the short course on home networking right here.

Part IV: Ten Helpful Hints on Windows XP

Magazine top ten lists can be great time-wasters in the grocery checkout line, but this part should be the opposite: Turn here for ten time-savers when exploring Windows XP.

Icons Used in This Book

Already seen Windows? Then you've probably noticed its *icons,* which are little pictures for starting various programs. The icons in this book fit right in. They're even a little easier to figure out:

 Watch out! This signpost warns you that pointless technical information is coming around the bend. Swerve away from this icon, and you'll be safe from the awful technical drivel.

 This icon alerts you about juicy information that makes computing easier: a tried-and-true method for keeping the cat from sleeping on top of the monitor, for instance.

 Don't forget to remember these important points. (Or at least dog-ear the pages so that you can look them up again a few days later.)

 The computer won't explode while you're performing the delicate operations associated with this icon. Still, wearing gloves and proceeding with caution is a good idea when this icon is near.

Oh Yeah, One Last Thing

Microsoft allows computer manufacturers to add and remove some programs when they install Windows XP to new PCs. But that doesn't mean you have to miss out on all the fun. Check out Microsoft's Web site (www.microsoft.com) for more information on getting any goodies I talk about but which you're missing.

By the way, if you want more of this Windows XP stuff, pick up a copy of *Windows XP For Dummies,* published by Wiley Publishing, Inc. That's the book all this information is based on.

Okay, you're all set to jump right in.

Part I
Getting to Know Windows XP

● ●

In This Part

▶ Taking a look at the Start menu and taskbar

▶ Finding out about the My Computer program

▶ Activating Windows XP

▶ Getting help and using System Restore

● ●

*W*indows XP may have gone through a major renovation, but some things never change. For example, the Start button is still the button that gets your computer to do what you want it to do. And the taskbar is still the main toolbar that you can't live without. This part gives you a fast look at how you can take advantage of the Start button's features and the taskbar's versatility to improve your overall Windows XP experience.

But wait, there's more. In this part, I demystify the not-so-mysterious My Computer program, show you how to make sure Microsoft knows that you've activated Windows XP, and explain how to use Windows XP's valuable Help system and System Restore if you find yourself in computer purgatory.

The Start Button's Reason to Live

The Start button lives on your taskbar, and it's always ready for action. By using the Start button, you can start programs, adjust the Windows XP settings, find help for sticky situations, or, thankfully, shut down Windows XP and get away from the computer for a while.

The little Start button is so eager to please, in fact, that it starts shooting out menus full of options as soon as you click it. Just click the button once, and the first layer of menus pops out, neatly labeled in Figure 1-1.

✔ The Start menu changes as you add programs to your computer. That change means that the Start menu on your friend's computer probably offers slightly different programs from the Start menu on your own computer.

✔ Save your files in your My Documents folder. Save your photos in your My Pictures folder. And save your music in your My Music folder. You can easily access each folder from the Start menu. And each folder is specially designed for its contents.

✔ See the little arrow by the words All Programs near the bottom left of the Start menu? Click the arrow, and another menu squirts out, listing more programs stored inside your computer.

✔ Windows graciously places your most frequently used programs along the left side of the Start menu. The Start menu in earlier versions of Windows displayed icons for the last ten *documents* you accessed.

Adjust settings here ─────────────────────────────────┐

Displays computers connected to your own computer ──┐ │

Displays computer's disk drives ──────────────┐ │ │

Click to access files by category ──────────┐ │ │ │

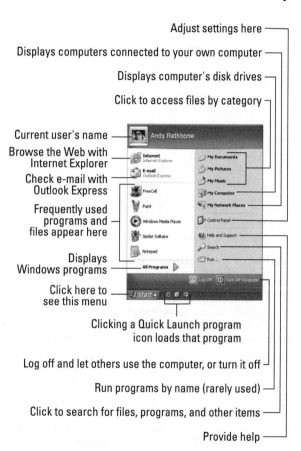

Current user's name ─── Andy Rathbone

Browse the Web with ─── Internet / Internet Explorer
Internet Explorer

Check e-mail with ─── E-mail / Outlook Express
Outlook Express

Frequently used ─── FreeCell / Paint / Windows Media Player / Spider Solitaire / Notepad
programs and
files appear here

Displays ─── All Programs
Windows programs

Click here to ─── start
see this menu

My Documents
My Pictures
My Music
My Computer
My Network Places
Control Panel
Help and Support
Search
Run...

Log Off   Turn Off Computer

Clicking a Quick Launch program
icon loads that program

Log off and let others use the computer, or turn it off ─┘

Run programs by name (rarely used) ─┘

Click to search for files, programs, and other items ─┘

Provide help ─┘

Figure 1-1: Click the taskbar's Start button to see a list of
options.

Starting a program from the Start button

This one's easy. Click the Start button, and the Start menu pops out of the button's head. If you see an icon for your desired program or file, click it, and Windows loads the program or file.

If your program isn't listed, though, click the words All Programs. Yet another menu pops up, this one listing the names of programs or folders full of programs.

If you see your program listed there, click the name. Wham! Windows XP kicks that program to the screen. If you don't see your program listed, try pointing at the tiny folders listed on the menu. New menus fly out of those folders, listing even more programs. When you finally spot your program's name, just click it.

Adding a program's icon to the Start menu

The Windows XP Start button works great — until you're hankering for something that's not listed on its menu. How do you add a favorite program's icon to the Start menu? Windows XP makes it easier than ever.

When you install a program, the program almost always adds itself to the Start menu automatically. Then it announces its presence to you and to all the other users of the computer.

To see the newly installed program, click the words All Programs, and a huge menu of additional programs appears. Windows XP highlights the newly installed program and usually places it in alphabetical order on the menu.

✔ There's another way to add a program to the Start menu. Windows XP adds icons for your five most-frequently used programs to the Start menu's left column. If you come across an icon or shortcut for a program that you'd like to appear there, right-click on the icon. Choose Pin to Start Menu from the menu that appears, and Windows places that icon in the left column of your Start menu.

✔ To get rid of unwanted icons from the Start menu's left column, right-click on the icons and choose Remove from This List; they disappear. Remember, though, the icons on the Start menu are just shortcuts. Removing the icon from the list doesn't remove the program from your computer.

The Way-Cool Taskbar

The Windows XP taskbar is a special program that keeps track of all your open programs. Shown in Figure 1-2, the taskbar normally lives along the bottom of your screen, although you can move it to any edge you want.

Click here to reveal hidden icons

Figure 1-2: The handy taskbar lists your currently running programs.

Sometimes the taskbar hides things. Click the little arrow near the clock (refer to Figure 1-2), and a few more icons might slide out.

Windows XP brings a whirlwind of new options for the lowly taskbar. Right-click on a blank part of the taskbar, and a menu appears. Choose the Properties option, and the Taskbar and Start Menu Properties dialog box appears.

Here's what the options in this dialog box mean. (You may need to click the Lock the Taskbar check box to remove its check mark before some of these options will work.)

Lock the Taskbar: Click in this box, and Windows XP "locks" the taskbar in place. You can't drag it to one edge of the window, drag it up to make it bigger, or drag it down beneath the edge of the screen.

Auto-Hide the Taskbar: Some people think the taskbar gets in the way. So, they drag it down below the bottom of the screen. (Try it.) Clicking in this box makes the taskbar automatically hide itself below the screen's bottom. Point the mouse at the screen's bottom, and the taskbar rises automatically from its grave.

Keep the Taskbar on Top of Other Windows: This option keeps the taskbar always visible, covering up any windows that may be low on the screen.

Group Similar Taskbar Buttons: When you open lots of windows and programs, the taskbar gets crowded. Windows accommodates the crowd by shrinking the buttons. Unfortunately, that means you can't read the buttons' names. This option groups similar windows under one button. When things get crowded, Windows groups all your Internet Explorer windows under one Internet Explorer button on the taskbar, for instance, as shown in Figure 1-3.

Figure 1-3: Select Group Similar Taskbar Buttons to save space on your taskbar by stacking similar buttons.

  Show Quick Launch: The tiny icons that live next to the taskbar's Start button make up the Quick Launch toolbar, which you turn on by clicking in this box. Try it — the Quick Launch toolbar places itty-bitty icons for Internet Explorer and Media Player next to the Start button for easy access. Just drag program icons to the Quick Launch bar to add them to it. (Drag the icons off to remove them.)

Show the Clock: You want to know when it's time to leave work, don't you?

Hide Inactive Icons: This option lets you hide those little icons — like the volume control, printer button, and other doodies — that begin hanging out by your clock. Click the Customize button to choose which icons should show up, which should hide, and which should appear only when they're being used.

Feel free to experiment with the taskbar, changing its size and position until it looks right for you. It won't break. After you set it up just the way you want, select the Lock the Taskbar check box described earlier in this list.

Why Is the My Computer Program So Frightening?

Windows needs a place to store your programs and files. So, it borrowed the file cabinet metaphor, translated it into light and airy Windows icons, and called it the My Computer program. My Computer shows the files and storage areas inside your computer, allowing you to copy or move them, rename them, or delete them.

 Everybody organizes his or her computer differently. To see how your computer has organized your files, click the Start menu and then click My Computer (the icon shown in the margin). Your My Computer window probably looks a little different from the one shown in Figure 1-4.

The My Computer program is a big panel of buttons — sort of an extension of your desktop. Here's a brief rundown on what those big icons along My Computer's right side mean.

 Files Stored on This Computer: Windows XP lets many people use the same computer, and everybody's files stay private. However, sometimes everybody wants to share information — letters from relatives, for instance. That's where the Shared Documents folder (shown in the margin) comes in.

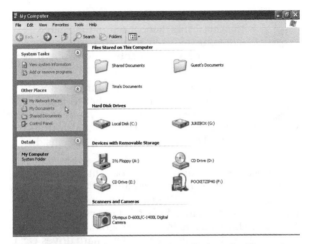

Figure 1-4: The My Computer window displays the files and storage areas inside your computer, allowing you to copy, rename, move, or delete them.

The Shared Documents folder contains files and folders accessible to everybody who uses the computer. To share things with other users of your computer, call up My Computer and store the information inside My Computer's Shared Documents folder. (Double-clicking any folder shows its contents.)

Two additional folders live inside the Shared Documents folder: Shared Music and Shared Pictures. Everybody using the computer may also access music and pictures stored in here.

If you don't want to share your information with other users, keep it out of the Shared Documents folder. Instead, store the information in your My Documents folder, accessible from the Start menu.

Notice two other folders in Figure 1-4, one belonging to Guest and the other to Tina? You see those folders because you're viewing the My Computer area of an administrator's account. The administrator can peek inside the files of any other user.

Hard Disk Drives: This one's not too difficult. It lists the hard drives installed on your computer. Double-clicking a folder here shows what's inside, but you rarely find much useful information. In fact, Windows often simply tells you to back off and look for programs on your Start menu, instead. Unlike files and folders, hard drives can't be moved to different areas.

Devices with Removable Storage: This area shows stuff you take in and out of your computer: floppy drives, CD-ROM drives, Iomega Jaz drives, and even MP3 players, if they're Windows XP compatible.

Scanners and Cameras: Digital cameras and scanners often appear down here, depending on their make and model.

Unlike files and folders, Hard Disk Drives, Devices with Removable Storage, and Scanners and Cameras can't be moved to different areas. They're stuck where they live in the My Computer area. To make them more accessible, you can place shortcuts to them on your desktop or any other convenient spot.

What's that Windows Explorer thing?

Although Windows almost always displays your files and folders in its My Computer program window, another program can help you examine your files and folders. My Computer only shows the contents of a single folder at a time. Windows Explorer, on the other hand, lets you see all your folders at the same time.

To load Windows Explorer from My Computer, click the Folders button on the toolbar at the top. A list of folders tacks itself onto My Computer's left side, turning it into Windows Explorer.

Some people prefer Windows Explorer's "view it all" method of displaying your computer's contents. Others prefer My Computer. There's no right or wrong way. Try them both and see which you prefer.

My Computer also includes several boxes along its left side. They serve mainly as shortcuts — pointers — that take you to other areas on your computer. The boxes change according to what you're viewing in My Computer. These choices appear when you first open My Computer, and here's what they mean. See Part II of this book for more info and shortcuts for moving around files in My Computer.

System Tasks: Both items listed here, View System Information and Add or Remove Programs, deal with your computer's innards. They're shortcuts to icons on Windows XP's Control Panel.

Other Places: Three of these items, My Network Places, My Documents, and Control Panel, are simply shortcuts to items that appear on your computer's Start menu.

I dunno why there's a shortcut to the Shared Documents folder here, because the Shared Documents folder already appears a few inches to the right, as you can see in Figure 1-4.

Details: Finally, something interesting. Click almost any icon in My Computer, and the Details window automatically displays information about that object: the date a file was created, for instance, or how much space it consumes.

Activating Windows XP

Here's a big secret: You don't really own Windows XP. Even when you buy Windows at the store, or it comes preinstalled on your new computer, it's not yours. No, the fine print says that only Microsoft owns Windows. You only own a license — permission — to run Windows on your computer. Worse than that, you're only granted permission to run Windows on a single computer.

In the past, many people bought one version of Windows — one for their desktop computer and one for their laptop. And why not? They either used their desktop computer or their laptop — they never used them both at the same time.

Windows XP changes that with its new Activation feature. When you install Windows XP, an annoying window pops up, asking you to "activate" your version of Windows. When you click the Activate button, Windows XP takes a "picture" of your computer's components, links it to the serial number on your copy of Windows XP, and sends that information to Microsoft over the Internet.

Then, if you or anybody else ever tries to install that same version of Windows on a different computer, Windows XP says you're using somebody else's version of Windows XP, and it won't work.

✔ Okay, what happens if you don't bother to activate a copy of Windows XP? It simply stops working after 30 days. The new Activation feature ensures that each copy of Windows XP will only work on a single computer. Even if Windows XP came preinstalled on your new computer, you can't take the bundled Windows XP CD and install it on another computer.

✔ No Internet connection? Then you must call Microsoft's toll-free number, talk to a customer service representative, and activate your copy of Windows by typing in a 25-number password.

✔ If you want to install Windows XP on several computers, it might be cheaper to purchase a special multi-version license, called a Microsoft License Pak.

✔ If you upgrade your computer — adding lots of new parts — Windows XP might think it's been installed on a new computer and stop working. The solution? You must call Microsoft's toll-free number and convince those folks that you're not trying to steal their software.

Using Windows' Help and Support Center

Although most Windows programs include an individu-
alized Help program, which you can access by clicking
Help from their menus, Windows XP also includes an
all-encompassing Help program. It helps with general
Windows questions, as well as your computer in general. To start using it, choose Help and Support from
the Start menu. The program rises to the screen, as
shown in Figure 1-5.

The Help and Support Center offers assistance in these
categories:

- **Pick a Help Topic:** Click these to see general
  information about a topic. Clicking Customizing
  Your Computer, for example, displays a list of
  things that you can change about your computer.

- **Ask for Assistance:** Stumped? Here are two
  ways of bringing in outside help. The Remote
  Assistance program lets you invite a savvier
  Windows XP user to connect to your computer
  through the Internet. When the Geek connects to
  your computer, he sees your desktop on his
  screen. He can walk you through problems, offer
  tutorials, and behave as if he were standing over
  your shoulder. If you're not into that kind of computer intimacy, try the other option through
  which you can contact Microsoft for help or
  connect to help sites through the Internet.

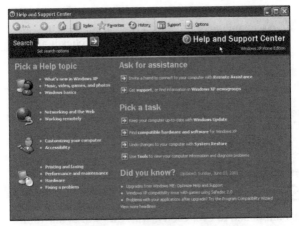

Figure 1-5: Windows' Help and Support Center offers assistance with Windows and your computer.

- ✔ **Pick a Task:** Microsoft placed the most commonly used items here. One click enables you to keep your computer up-to-date, find Windows XP–compatible parts for your computer, restore your computer back to a time when it worked well (see the next section for more on System Restore), and run diagnostic tools to view information and test your computer.

- ✔ **Did You Know?:** Windows XP tosses little updated tips here. You may just get lucky and spot one that's useful.

For best results, start your quest for help by glancing at the Pick a Help Topic area. If your troublesome spot is listed here, click it and begin narrowing down the search for pertinent information.

If that doesn't help, use the Search box at the page's top. Type in a key word or two describing your problem and click the green arrow next to the Search box. Click any of the suggested topics to see if they solve your problem.

Restoring Calm with System Restore

It's happened to everybody: Windows works fine until something happens; then it's all over. For instance, you delete a file, and Windows begins hitting you up with an ugly error message each time it loads. Or you install a new program, which promptly disconnects your scanner, digital camera, modem, or all three.

Wouldn't you love to go back in time to when Windows worked right? Thank goodness Windows XP lets you turn back the clock with a few clicks on a program called System Restore.

Every day, Windows stores a "picture" of your computer's settings on your hard disk. If your computer begins acting weird, load up System Restore, click the last day your computer did work fine, and System Restore goes back in time to reset your computer to its settings from back when it worked correctly. Whew! Here's how to head back to happier times:

1. **Save any open files, close any loaded programs, and load System Restore.**

   Choose Start, click All Programs, and begin weaving your way through the menus: Choose Accessories, select System Tools, and click System Restore.

2. **Click Restore My Computer to an Earlier Time and then click Next.**

3. **Click a calendar date when your computer worked well and then click Next.**

   Yesterday is your best bet. But if the symptoms have been going on for longer, choose a day *before* your computer began having problems.

4. **Make sure you've saved any open files and then click Next.**

   Your computer grumbles a bit and then restarts. System Restore resets your computer to earlier settings when everything worked fine; you won't lose any work that you've saved.

   System Restore is completely reversible. If your computer winds up in even worse shape, load System Restore and choose a different date.

Before installing a program or any new computer toys, load System Restore and create a restore point in case the installation is a disaster. To do that, open System Restore; then, in Step 2 of the preceding steps, select the System Restore button marked Create a Restore Point. That tells Windows to take a snapshot of its current condition so that you can return to it if things go downhill.

If you restore your computer to a time before you installed some new hardware or software, those items may not function properly. If they're not working correctly, reinstall them.

Part II
Discovering Windows XP and Multimedia

. . . .

In This Part

▶ Using a digital camera or scanner with Windows XP

▶ Viewing pictures

▶ Taking a look at Media Player

▶ Creating CDs and WMAs

▶ Making Media Player create MP3s and play DVDs

▶ Moving music or video to an MP3 player or Pocket PC

. . . .

*W*ith Windows XP, you're missing out if you're not using all of the digital video and audio technology at your fingertips. If you're interested in creating and sharing digital pictures, listening to and recording music, and sharing digital files with your MP3 player or Pocket PC, this part gets you started.

Using Your Digital Camera and Scanner

 Windows usually detects scanners and new-fangled digital cameras when they're first turned on and plugged into your computer. Other times, scanners and cameras come with their own installation software. Still other cameras need to be formally introduced to Windows — just click the Scanners and Cameras icon in the Control Panel's Printers and Other Hardware category and then click the Add an Imaging Device option.

Windows brings up its Installation Wizard. Click the manufacturer's name on the window's left side and choose the model on the right. Choose the correct COM port if you know where you've plugged in the device; otherwise, choose Automatic Port Detection. If you've turned on your camera or scanner and plugged in its cable correctly, Windows should recognize it and place an icon for it in both your My Computer area and your Control Panel's Scanners and Camera area.

 Unfortunately, the installation of cameras and scanners doesn't always work this easily. If yours isn't automatically accepted, use the software that came with your scanner or camera. It should still work — you just won't be able to use Windows XP's built-in software.

To grab the pictures from your installed camera, turn it on and open your My Pictures folder (you can access the My Pictures folder from the Start menu). Choose

Get Pictures from Camera or Scanner. Windows recognizes the pictures and displays tiny thumbnail pictures of them across the screen.

> To pick and choose from the keepers, hold down Ctrl while clicking the good ones. In fact, because many cameras take such a l-o-o-o-n-g time to download, this trick comes in handy for quick grabs. Save the pictures in your My Pictures folder.

Viewing Previews of Your Pictures

Windows XP has made it easier than ever to peek inside your graphics files. Instead of displaying a folder full of bland icons, Windows XP transforms each icon into a thumbnail-sized preview of the file's contents. Best yet, the previews are all done automatically.

Although Windows XP displays the thumbnail view automatically when it spies digital pictures in a folder, keeping your pictures in your My Pictures folder is best. That makes it easier to find them later and keeps them separate from the pictures stored by other users of your computer.

> Choose Filmstrip from the folder's View menu to see a filmstrip of all your pictures, with the currently selected picture displayed above. (Click a picture to see its properties, as shown in Figure 2-1.)

Figure 2-1: Windows XP displays your photos in the folder, making it much easier to locate them.

Looking Over the Windows XP Media Player

For years, computers could only cut loose with a rude beep, which they issued to harass confused users who pressed the wrong keys. The Windows XP Media Player changes all that, handling fancy videos, Internet radio stations, CDs, DVDs, MP3s, and more.

Media Player's performance depends entirely upon how much money you paid for your computer — or how much money your computer has absorbed since you first plopped it on your desk.

That's because Media Player is nothing more than a big, fancy package of buttons. Before you can use those buttons to do anything, you need to connect your computer to features such as speakers, sound cards, CD burners, CD/DVD drives, the Internet, and MP3 players. Pressing the right buttons calls these right things into action and tells the computer what to do with them.

Figure 2-2, which explains some of the zillions of Media Player buttons, shows Media Player when it first loads. (If you get lost amid all those buttons, just rest your mouse pointer over any button, and Windows XP gives you a hint.)

✔ You need a sound card and speakers or headphones before you can hear anything. Luckily, most new computers come with preinstalled sound cards; many come with speakers, as well.

✔ A CD-ROM drive is essential for playing CDs or creating WMA (Windows Media Audio) files. You need a Read/Write CD drive, too, so that you can burn CDs of your favorite music. Many new computers come with those included, as well.

✔ You need an Internet connection to listen to Internet radio or search the Web for videos or other media content. Faster is better. In fact, most Internet videos look pretty tiny or grainy if you're using a dial-up connection.

✔ Windows XP's Media Player uses WMA compatibility to decide whether it will transfer files to a portable MP3 player. If your portable player can't handle WMA files, Media Player probably won't transfer *any* files to it. But if the player handles WMA files along with MP3 files, Media Player can usually transfer both WMA and MP3 files to your player.

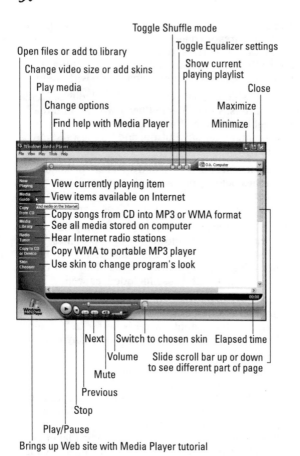

Figure 2-2: Rest your mouse over any button, and Windows XP explains its purpose.

Burning your own CDs

Windows XP lets you burn your music onto writeable CDs in two *very* different ways.

First, it can dump files onto a CD for sheer storage. For instance, you can copy more than 150 MP3 or WMA files onto a single CD. Just open My Computer, right-click on the files, choose Send To, and select your CD drive. Next, open your writeable CD drive in My Computer and choose Write These Files to CD. (In fact, this trick works for any files that you want to copy to a CD, not just music files.)

Second, Windows XP lets you create standard music CDs — CDs containing a dozen or so songs that play back in your home or car CD player. By mixing songs from various albums, you can create your own greatest hits CD containing your favorite songs.

To store a dozen or so songs on a CD for playing on your home or car's CD player, follow these instructions:

1. **Insert your blank CD into your writeable CD drive.**

   When the helpful little message pops up, click Take No Action. Media Player handles the details.

2. **Open Media Player and click Copy to CD or Device.**

   (This button is one of the buttons along the left side of Media Player.) Media Player shows a window split in two. One side displays the files you'd like to copy to the CD; the other side shows the CD. (Both sides are empty because you haven't selected any files, and you're copying to a blank CD.)

3. Click Media Player's Media Library button.

Click an album containing songs that you want to copy to the CD; its songs appear on Media Player's right side.

4. Right-click on the desired song and choose Copy to Audio CD.

Each time you click a song and choose Copy to Audio CD, Media Player immediately shows you the window you see in Step 2, with your currently chosen file on the Music to Copy list. Media Player keeps track of each song's length, listing the total at the list's bottom.

Why does Media Player care? Because CDs hold only 74 or 80 minutes of music. If you try to stuff too many songs onto the CD, Media Player displays next to some songs' names the message Will Not Fit. To remove songs that won't fit, click the check-marked box next to their names.

5. Click Copy Music, the little red button near the upper-right corner.

Now it's time to move away from your computer for a while. Windows must convert the files into the proper CD format, and that takes about ten minutes. Then Windows needs a half hour or so to copy the music onto the CD — and Microsoft warns you not to fiddle with your computer while creating a CD because Media Player could "stop functioning."

✔ Media Player copies to both CD-R and CD-RW discs. Many stereos choke on CD-RW discs, so you're best off with the CD-R discs.

✔ When storing songs onto your hard drive, Media Player compresses them into WMA format, losing some quality in the process. To let Media Player work with the best-quality recordings when creating CDs, use the highest quality level possible when ripping songs onto your hard drive. (Set the quality level by choosing Options from the Tools menu, clicking the Copy Music tab, and sliding the tab to Best Quality.)

Playing DVDs

Microsoft raves about how Media Player plays DVDs. But that's a lie. Windows XP can't play DVDs right out of the box. See, even though you've bought a Windows XP computer, a DVD drive, and a DVD, you need something else: special software called a *decoder*. This bit of software, called a *codec* because it converts one format to another, enables your computer to translate numbers on a disc into videos of galloping horses on the screen.

Unfortunately, Windows XP doesn't come with a DVD codec, so you must pick up one somewhere else. Where? Well, most computers with DVD drives come with DVD-playing software — a little box with its own little controls. That software installs its own DVD codec in Windows, and Media Player simply borrows that. But if you don't have DVD-playing software, there's nothing to borrow, and Media Player ignores your DVDs.

✔ If you choose Windows Media Player instead of your third-party DVD player to watch DVDs, the controls are pretty much the same as they are for playing CDs.

✔ You probably need to update your DVD software
so that it will work under Windows XP. Otherwise
your DVD software won't work under Media
Player, either. Head for the Web site of your DVD
player's manufacturer and look for a Windows XP
patch or upgrade. If you're lucky, the manufacturer won't charge you for the upgrade. Some
companies, however, make you buy a new version.

DVD stands for Digital Video Disc, Digital
Versatile Disc, and Dick Van Dyke.

Creating WMAs

Media Player lets you copy songs from your CDs onto
your computer, but only in the WMA format. That's too
bad because MP3 is much more popular and is sup-
ported by every portable MP3 player. Microsoft hopes
WMA will catch on because of Microsoft's marketing
muscle. Plus, WMA files are half the size of MP3 files.

Before you copy files, you must tell Media Player where
to store them and what format to use. Choose Options
from Media Player's Tools menu and click the Copy
Music tab.

To save space, store your music in your computer's
Shared Music folder so that every user can hear it:
Click the Change button, click My Computer, click
Shared Documents, and choose Shared Music. Click OK
to save your changes.

Make sure no check mark is in the Protect Content box.
Then you're ready to copy the songs from a CD onto
your computer, where you can listen to them, catalog
them, or copy them directly to MP3 players and
Pocket PCs.

1. **Log onto the Internet.**

   Although not essential, an Internet connection automatically fills in the CD's song titles while Media Player creates your WMAs. Using the Internet is a great timesaver and helps avoid embarrassing misspellings.

2. **Load Media Player.**

3. **Insert your audio CD into your computer and click the Stop Play button.**

   Media Player will probably begin playing the songs, but it copies faster if the CD doesn't play.

4. **Click the Copy from CD button.**

   After you click the Copy from CD button, Media Player shows all the CD's song titles, which are all selected.

5. **Remove the check marks from any titles that you don't want to copy.**

6. **Click Copy Music, the red button near the top.**

   Media Player begins copying the selected song(s) from the CD to your hard drive in your chosen format. That's it.

To listen to your newly copied files, click the Media Library button and find your CD listed under the Album section. Click the CD's name, and all the copied songs appear on Media Player's right-hand side.

Just like Windows XP doesn't include a codec to play DVD files, it doesn't include a codec for creating MP3 files. The solution? You need third-party MP3 software that includes an MP3

encoder. If Media Player feels that the encoder meets the specifications of Microsoft, it borrows that program's encoder in order to copy MP3s. (Choose Options from the Tools menu and click the Copy Music tab to choose your file format, WMA or MP3.)

Moving music or video to an MP3 player or Pocket PC

Start the easy way: Turn off Media Player's WMA licensing features when you copy files from a CD. (Choose Options from the Tools menu, click the Copy Music tab, and remove any check mark from the Protect Content check box.) That way your WMA files will play back on nearly every MP3 player on the market.

Media Player can copy files straight from your Media Library into your MP3 player or Pocket PC. However, it only works that way with some of the newer devices, such as Iomega's HipZip, Creative's Nomad II, the Rio 600 and 800, and others.

Here's how to copy music or video to your MP3 player or Pocket PC:

1. **Connect your device to your computer.**

   Some devices connect through a serial cable; others use a USB or parallel port. Some connect a FlashCard reader to your PC.

2. **Turn on the device.**

   A window usually pops up, asking whether Windows should play the music files on the device, or open the device's contents in a folder so that you can view it. Click Cancel because you don't need either option to copy files using Media Player.

Copy to CD or Device **3. Click the Copy to CD or Device button.**

Media Player connects with your device. (Press F5 if it has trouble finding your device.) Media Player shows the device's current contents on the left and your Media Player's songs on the right.

4. Decide what to copy to your device.

Click the arrow in the Music to Copy drop-down list box, and a long list drops down. You can select music by artist, CD title, and genre. Or choose All Audio from the list to see *all* your available songs.

The songs that you choose appear in the window below. They're all checked, and Media Player keeps a size total so that you know what songs will and won't fit. To uncheck them all, click the little check box next to the word Title. Then you can choose songs separately by clicking in their boxes.

To erase songs on your current player, right-click on their titles and choose Delete from Playlist.

5. Click the red Copy Music button near Media Player's upper-right corner.

Media Player dutifully copies the selected songs into your portable device.

✔ If you see the message An Error Occurred, it probably means that you're trying to pack too big of a file onto your player, and there's not enough room. Choose a smaller file and see if that fits in the remaining space.

✔ The quickest way to move files to a player is to buy a CompactFlash card reader and connect it to your computer. Then copy the WMA or MP3 files to the card reader using My Computer. Transfer sessions take seconds instead of minutes.

✔ Media Player also copies videos into Pocket PCs, if you have one of those little goodies. Beware, though: Copying videos can take a *long* time. In fact, unless your music player or Pocket PC connects to your computer with a USB port, the transfer could take 20 minutes or more.

✔ When copying tunes to your portable player or Pocket PC, save space by encoding your WMA files at 64 Kbps. Your files consume half the size of MP3 files and still sound good enough for the streets. To change the rate, choose Options from the Tools menu. Click the Copy Music tab and slide the quality setting bar to the 64 Kbps setting.

✔ WMA handles low encoding rates much better than MP3. That's why a 64 Kbps WMA file sounds much better than an MP3 file at 64 Kbps.

Part III
Setting Up a Windows XP Network at Home

● ●

In This Part

▶ Setting up user accounts for everyone in the family

▶ Using the built-in firewall

▶ Setting up a home network

● ●

*W*indows XP's new User Accounts feature makes it possible for everyone in your family to use the computer under a unique name and password — keeping personal files safe from outsiders. And if you like to cruise the Internet, then you're probably cautious about hackers. And why shouldn't you be? That's why Windows XP also contains a firewall that can keep bad files and bad people from getting to you through your PC. Windows XP also happens to be very network-friendly. You can connect all your computers (and printers, scanners, and so on) and share files between them. Not bad, eh?

In a nutshell, Windows XP is secure. In fact, the folks over at Microsoft went beyond the call of duty. This part gets you up to speed on how Windows XP's security updates help keep your computer — and your family — in safe hands.

Setting Up User Accounts

If you're the only person using your computer, you won't care about this. But if your family computer has a line around it like the bathroom of the *Brady Bunch*, then user accounts are for you.

When everybody has an individual user account, it's as if everybody has his or her own computer. Windows XP treats everybody differently — user accounts are not all grouped together on the same desktop. If one person changes the menus around, she has only changed the menus on her own account. The next person to use the computer finds the same menus he has always used.

Windows XP dishes out three types of user accounts: Administrator, Limited, and Guest. Who cares? Well, each type of account gets to do different functions on the computer. If the computer were an apartment building, the administrator would be the manager, the limited accounts would be the tenants, and guests would only get to drop by and use the bathroom in the lobby.

In computer lingo, that means the administrator controls the entire computer, deciding who gets to use it and what they can do on it. Limited accounts can access most of the areas of the computer, but they can't make any big changes to it. And guests, well, they can use the computer, but because the computer doesn't recognize them by name, their actions are tightly restricted.

> ✔ On a computer that's running Windows XP Home, the owner usually holds the administrator account. He or she then sets up accounts for other household members, changing their accounts when needed, fixing lost passwords, and

if desired, peeking into other users' files. Here's the important part: Only administrators can install software and change the computer's hardware.

✔ In a family, the parents usually hold administrator accounts, the kids usually have limited accounts, and the babysitter logs in using the guest account.

✔ Administrators should create *limited* accounts for people who use the computer on a regular basis. Windows XP then keeps track of the way each limited account member prefers his or her computer to be set up.

✔ Administrators should create a single *guest* account for people the computer doesn't need to recognize. Guests can't do much more than use the computer as a terminal, much like one in a library. Guests can use the programs, for example, but they can't change any settings, much less install programs or burn CDs.

When you install Windows XP, the software automatically grants administrator status to every account you create. Be sure to change these accounts to limited or guest status unless you trust those people to handle your computer wisely.

Switching quickly between users

Switching users is fast and easy. While holding down the Windows key (it's usually between your keyboard's Ctrl and Alt keys), press the letter L. Wham! The Welcome screen pops up, letting another person use the computer for a while.

- If you don't like the Windows key, use the mouse to switch users: Click the Start button and click Log Off from the bottom of the menu. After the new window appears, click Switch User. The Welcome screen appears.

  - Microsoft touts this feature as *Fast User Switching*, or *FUS* in the trade.

- If Fast User Switching doesn't work on your computer, the administrator may have turned it off (see the next section).

  - Choosing Log Off rather than using Fast User Switching is often better, especially for computers without a lot of memory. Programs automatically shut down after users log off the computer, and the computer runs faster for the next user. If you use Fast User Switching, the computer must juggle unsaved settings and open programs, leading to more overhead.

Creating, deleting, or changing a user account

Only administrators may create or delete user accounts. Sorry. If you don't see your name on the Welcome screen, you must log on as a guest. (And some computers don't even offer a guest account. That's up to the administrator, too.)

If you're an administrator (and if you're not, don't bother reading any further), feel free to create a limited user account for everybody who's going to use your computer. That gives them just enough control over the computer to keep them from bugging you all the time, yet it keeps them from accidentally deleting any important files.

To create, change, or delete a user account, click the Start button, choose the Control Panel, and select User Accounts. A window pops up, as shown in Figure 3-1, that's seen only by administrators. Here's a rundown on the different tasks available.

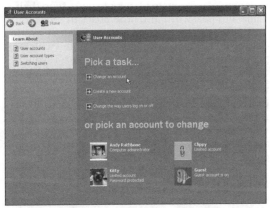

Figure 3-1: Only administrators can choose the Control Panel's User Accounts icon to change, create, or delete user accounts.

Change an Account: The most encompassing of the options, this lets you change an account's name, picture, password, or type. Click here to delete an account, as well.

Create a New Account: Click here to create accounts for other computer users. You choose a name and whether the user is to have an administrator or limited account.

Change the Way Users Log On and Off: This one's a little more complicated, because it brings up two options, described here:

✔ **Use the Welcome Screen:** Normally, people log on by clicking their names on the Welcome screen. Removing the check mark in this box turns off the Welcome screen. Instead, people must type their name and password into little boxes in order to log on. Why? This method is more secure — without the Welcome screen, nobody can tell which people have accounts on the computer. Turning off the Welcome screen also turns off Fast User Switching, described next.

✔ **Use Fast User Switching:** Windows XP usually lets users switch back and forth quickly and easily. When they switch back on, their open programs are just the way they left them. Removing the check mark in this box turns off the Fast User Switching for all users. Instead, they must log off, saving their work in the process, before another user may log on.

Securing Your PC with the Windows XP Firewall

My cable modem is constantly connected to the Internet, so it's no surprise that somebody tries to break into my computer at least a dozen times a day. No, a person isn't sitting at his computer, typing at the keyboard, and trying to find a way inside. These people run easy-to-find hacker programs that automatically scan thousands of computers, looking for one that's not secure.

If you're on the Internet, these hackers could be knocking on your door, as well — especially if you run a network or have a cable modem. To keep the bad guys out but let the good ones in, you need a *firewall* that filters the information that's going into your computer and keeps your computer invisible to the programs that search for unsecure computers.

Firewall software sits between your computer and the Internet, acting as a door. It lets you decide what software can access your computer, and when. Windows XP comes with a built-in firewall. To activate it, follow these steps:

1. **Open the Start menu, right-click on My Network Places, and choose Properties.**

2. **Right-click on the connection you want to protect and choose Properties.**

   If you're using a dial-up account, for instance, right-click on that icon. If you're using a network in your home or office, right-click on the Local Area Connection. Either way, choose Properties.

3. **Click the Advanced tab and click the box to activate the Windows XP firewall.**

If you're running a network and using the Internet Connection Sharing feature to enable all the networked computers to share the modem, the firewall should only be activated on the host computer — the computer that's actually connected to the Internet. (See the next section for more on networks.)

Skip the Rest of This Unless You Have or Want a Network

A *network* is just two or more computers that have been connected so that they can share information. But computer networks have more subtleties than nervous high schoolers on their first date.

For example, how do you tell if a computer is on a network? Who's allowed on the network? Which computers are on the network? Are all parts of Computer A available to Computer B? Should networked computers be allowed to kiss without passwords? All these technical decisions need to be made beforehand, usually by the network administrator.

Computers aren't the only elements that you can network. You can put printers, modems, CD-ROM drives, USB ports, CompactFlash card readers, and nearly anything else on a network, as well. No need to buy bunches of stuff for each computer; they can all share.

Windows XP divvies up its attention quite well. It lets all the networked computers share a single Internet connection, for instance, and everybody can be online *at the same time*. Everyone can share a single printer, too.

Letting the Network Setup Wizard set up your network

Whoopee! After you've installed the cards and cables, the Windows Network Setup Wizard takes over the rest of the arduous tasks. Be sure to run the wizard on your most powerful computer and make that computer the one that connects to the Internet.

Now, turn on all your computers, printers, and external modems and then connect your computer to the Internet. Ready? Here's how to summon the wizard to complete the network finalities:

1. **Start the Network Setup Wizard and click the Next button.**

   Click the Start button, choose My Network Places, and choose Set Up a Home or Small Office Network from the Network Tasks area along the left. The Network Setup Wizard rises to the screen, ready for you to click Next.

2. **Read the screen and click Next.**

   The Network Setup Wizard brings your network to life, examining everything connected to it and placing appropriate network icons on your computer. That's why turning everything on is important, as the wizard requests. After you click Next, the wizard looks for your Internet connection.

3. **Tell the wizard about your Internet connection and click Next.**

   Specifically, the wizard needs to know whether your computer connects directly to the Internet, or if it will connect to the Internet through a different computer on the network. Because you're running this wizard on the computer that connects to the Internet, choose the first option.

4. **Choose your Internet connection from the list, if asked, and click Next.**

5. **Type a name and description for your computer and click Next.**

6. **If the settings look correct, click Next.**

Windows XP lists the settings that it will use and asks for your okay. If you click Next, Windows XP checks out the Internet connection and lets other networked computers share it. It automatically installs a protective firewall, described earlier in the part. And it starts setting up the network. (Give it a few minutes.)

7. **If your network includes Windows 98 or Windows 95 computers, create a Home Networking Setup disk and click Next.**

   If any of your networked computers use those older versions of Windows, create the Network Setup disk by clicking the Create Disk button. (You need a floppy.)

   Ignore this step if you're networking all Windows XP computers. You can insert your Windows XP CD into those computers, choose Perform Additional Tasks, and select Set Up Home or Small Office Networking.

8. **Click Finish.**

   That should do the trick.

✔ The wizard does a reasonably good job of casting its spells on your computers. If the computers are all connected correctly and restarted, chances are they'll wake up in bondage with each other. If they don't, try restarting them all again.

✔ Your newly networked Windows XP computers should list currently shared folders in their My Network Places areas. Unless you've shared additional files on your own, you'll probably see a single folder called Shared Documents that contains My Music and My Pictures.

✔ To run the wizard on Windows 95 or 98 computers that aren't running Windows XP, insert your Network Setup disk into the computer you want to network. Open My Computer, double-click your floppy drive, and double-click the file named netsetup. The computer asks a few questions, tweaks itself, and reboots. (Just run the Network Wizard on networked Windows Me computers, if Windows XP didn't already set them up.)

✔ All of your networked computers should now be able to share any shared files, your modem connection, and any printers.

✔ If everything doesn't proceed as merrily as described here, don't worry. Networking *will* work. However, you need to make some more advanced tweaks that I don't have the space to describe here. Pick up a copy of Brian Livingston's *Windows XP Secrets,* published by Wiley Publishing, Inc. (It's around 1,200 pages.)

How do I make the network work?

Windows XP can connect to bunches of other computers through a home network, and, luckily, that makes it pretty easy to grab files from other people's computers. After the network's running, you'll be running right alongside it. There isn't much new to learn.

 See the My Network Places icon on your computer's Start menu (and shown in the margin)? That icon is the key to all the computers currently connected to your computer.

Double-click that icon, and a window appears, as shown in Figure 3-2. Your windows naturally differ because you have different computers. (And the computers probably have different names, too.) Figure 3-2, for instance, shows all the disk drives on other computers that connect to this one through a network.

Double-click the folder of the computer that you want to peek inside, and a new window appears, showing the contents of the folder on that computer — even though it might be in another room, in another office, or on another continent.

Figure 3-2: Double-click the desktop's My Network Places icon to see which places you can access on the network.

 To see all the computers currently linked to your computer, click View Workgroup Computers from the Network Tasks menu along the window's left side. Windows XP shows you the names of all the currently available computers.

✔ When viewing another computer's files, everything works just like it does on your own computer. Feel free to point and click inside the other computer's folders. To copy files back and forth, just drag and drop them to and from your computer's window to the other computer's window. (Sometimes a computer requires a password, however, so you'll have to ask the computer's owner for permission.)

✔ When you use a network to delete something from another networked computer — or somebody uses the network to delete a file from *your* computer — it's gone. It doesn't go into the Recycle Bin. Be careful, especially because the network administrator can often tell who deleted the file.

Part IV
Ten Helpful Hints on Windows XP

• •

In This Part
▶ Finding quick ways out of common quagmires
▶ Dragging around files with the My Computer program

• •

*W*hether your computer lives in solitude in your living room or mingles with other computers on a network, Windows XP looks and acts pretty much the same, so you can count on finding your way around with any or all of the ten tips in this chapter.

Five Tricks for Quick Answers

When you're not quite sure how to proceed in Windows XP from where you are, or when you just want to tidy up the screen a bit, one of the following tidbits may come in handy:

> ✔ **Pause for thought (and help):** Don't know what a certain button does in a program? Rest your mouse pointer over the button for a few seconds. A helpful box often pops up to explain the button's purpose.

- ✔ **Help shortcut:** If you're baffled, try pressing F1, that function key on your keyboard's upper-left corner. A help window appears, often bringing hints about your current problem.

- ✔ **See all open windows at once:** To quickly organize the windows on the desktop, click the taskbar's clock with your *right* mouse button. When the menu appears, click one of the Tile options, and all your open windows neatly tile across the screen. Or click Cascade to cascade the windows across the screen like a waterfall of cards.

- ✔ **Tidy up folder contents:** To keep icons organized in neat rows across a folder, right-click on the folder's background. When the menu pops up, choose Auto Arrange from the Arrange Icons menu.

- ✔ **Take the Tour:** For a brief look at what Windows XP can do, choose All Programs from the Start button, and choose Tour Windows XP from the Accessories menu.

Can't find a file you thought was open? Windows XP's built-in Task Manager keeps a master list of everything that's happening on your screen (even the invisible stuff), making it a prime detective for locating hidden windows. Pressing Ctrl, Alt, and Delete simultaneously brings up the Task Manager which lists all currently running programs when you click the Applications tab. Your missing window is somewhere on the list. When you spot the runaway window, click its name, and click the

Switch To button along the Task Manager's bottom. Your wayward window whisks itself to the forefront.

Five Filing Tips with My Computer

If you want to remember how to copy or move files in the My Computer program, you can hold down the right mouse button while dragging and then choose Copy Here or Move Here from the menu. Or you can practice using the five quick and easy methods explained in Table 4-1 until they become old hat.

Table 4-1: Copying and Moving Files with My Computer

To Do This . . .	Do This . . .
Copy a file to another location on the *same* disk drive	Hold down Ctrl and drag the file there.
Copy a file to a *different* disk drive	Drag it there.
Move a file to another location on the same disk drive	Drag it there.
Move a file to a different disk drive	Hold down Shift and drag the file there.
Make a shortcut while dragging a file	Hold down Ctrl+Shift and drag the file there.

To share a file with all the users of your computer, open My Computer and copy the file into your Shared Documents folder.

Bonus tip: Shutting down Windows XP

If you decide to turn off your computer, don't just head for the off switch. First, tell Windows XP about your plans. Windows XP needs to prepare itself for shutdown, or it may accidentally eat some of your important information. To prevent that disaster, click the Start button, choose the Turn Off Computer command, and ponder the choices Windows XP places on the screen:

- ✔ Stand By: Save your work before choosing this option: Windows XP doesn't save your work automatically. Instead, it lets your computer doze for a bit to save power, but the computer wakes up at the touch of a button.

- ✔ Turn Off: Clicking here tells Windows XP to put away all your programs and to make sure that you've saved all your important files. Then it turns off your computer and most of the newer monitors. Use this option when you're done for the day.

- ✔ Restart: Here, Windows saves your work and prepares your computer to be shut off. However, it then restarts your computer. Use this option when installing new software, changing settings, or trying to stop Windows XP from doing something weird.

- ✔ Hibernate: Only offered on some computers, this option works much like Shut Down. It saves your work and turns off your computer. However, when turned on again, your computer presents your desktop just as you left it: Open programs and windows appear in the same place.

Remember, if you're done with the computer but other people might want to use it, just click Log Off from the Start menu: Windows XP saves your work and brings up the Welcome screen, allowing other people to log on and play video games.

ORDER TODAY!

FREE GIFT/SAMPLE ISSUE COUPON

Cut coupon and mail to: PC World, 501 Second Street, San Francisco, CA 94107

YES! Please rush my FREE CD wallet and my FREE sample issue of PC World! If I like PC WORLD, I'll honor your invoice and receive 11 more issues (12 in all) for just $19.97—that's 76% off the newsstand rate .

No Cost Examination Guarantee

If I decide PC WORLD is not for me, I'll write "cancel" on the invoice and owe nothing. The sample issue and CD wallet are mine to keep no matter what.

Name

Company

Address

City   State   Zip

Email

PC WORLD